GET MORE LAUGHS FROM YOUR LAUGHS

GET MORE LAUGHS FROM YOUR LAUGHS

◆

How to Be Funny

Robert W Klamm

iUniverse, Inc.
New York Lincoln Shanghai

GET MORE LAUGHS FROM YOUR LAUGHS
How to Be Funny

Copyright © 2005 by R. W. Klamm

All rights reserved. No part of this book may be used or reproduced by any means, graphic, electronic, or mechanical, including photocopying, recording, taping or by any information storage retrieval system without the written permission of the publisher except in the case of brief quotations embodied in critical articles and reviews.

iUniverse books may be ordered through booksellers or by contacting:

iUniverse
2021 Pine Lake Road, Suite 100
Lincoln, NE 68512
www.iuniverse.com
1-800-Authors (1-800-288-4677)

Art Work by Theo Boyd

ISBN-13: 978-0-595-37373-4 (pbk)
ISBN-13: 978-0-595-81770-2 (ebk)
ISBN-10: 0-595-37373-9 (pbk)
ISBN-10: 0-595-81770-X (ebk)

Printed in the United States of America

To my wife, Berniece, who has taken on my own hopes and dreams, and made them a part of hers. She has dealt patiently with the tedium that goes with putting any book together, dealing with the details and drudgery that I have been unable or unwilling to do for myself. She is the Gracie Allen to my George Burns.

Contents

FOREWORD ix

INTRODUCTION xi

Chapter 1   IT ONLY HURTS WHEN I DON'T LAUGH 1

Chapter 2   PUTTING TWO & TWO FOUR-GETHER 8

Chapter 3   NUTS AND BOLTS MAKE ME SCREWY . . . 15

Chapter 4   IT'S THE PAUSE THAT IMPRESSES! 29

Chapter 5   PRESS SHIFT F5 FOR CHARACTER ALIGNMENT 39

IN CONCLUSION 50

Appendix 51

ABOUT THE AUTHOR 53

FOREWORD

They say that comedy is a serious business. And my good friend Bob (R. W. Klamm) is really serious about comedy. The book that you have in your hand, dear reader was written for those who want to create laughter; no matter if you are a professional or not.

The contents of this book show you how deeply and passionately Bob studied the subject. Every topic has been analyzed and explained with accuracy and precision. You'll find: Comedy Contradiction, Exaggeration, Rules of Physical Action, Punch-line Sentence Structure, Dual Reality, Innocence and Believability, Timing and the Pause, Building Your Own Comedy Characterization, plus much more. More than that, you will find comic devices with funny examples and you'll have fun with the game-like exercises included with each chapter.

In a few words, you'll be the lucky one if you study the material assembled between these two covers. You'll learn how to use humor to light up the shadows in your life, heal the spirit, lower your blood pressure, fight the traffic and face every day problems with a smile. Whether you become a stand-up comedian with an HBO special of your own or not, you'll be richer and a better performer for the effort.

Thanks Bob…laughter is the best medicine. With this book you'll create a lot of smiles and you will heal a lot of people.

Aldo Colombini

Aldo Colombini
Mamma Mia Magic
805-499-3161
Fax 805-499-3561
acmagic@mindspring.com
www.mammamiamagic.com

INTRODUCTION

I was a basket case when it came to doing comedy, until I discovered these techniques. In 1959 I became drama coach for a Kansas City, Missouri High School; and was looking forward to doing good things of great stature. We did *Diary of Anne Frank* our first year. It was received with great enthusiasm as an artistic triumph, at a time when most high schools were doing only third-rate comedies, written primarily for high school consumption. Drama was my forte. I knew absolutely nothing about doing comedy.

Quite naturally, the kids wanted to do comedy as well as serious stuff. I was scared to death. I stalled as long as possible. When I finally gave in, I realized it would be sure-death to tackle a third rate script. We had better do something from an author who had been proven on Broadway.

We settled on *You Can't Take It with You*, a Pulitzer prize-winning comedy by Kaufman and Hart, with loads of zany characters. There was no doubt of its greatness. Our high school actors loved it; and with those wild characters, who could miss? Just treat it like any other good play.

With such a logical approach, I figured it for a shoe-in. The audience figured it for just plain dumb.

I knew if I were to keep my job—or at least the respect of my students—I would have to learn to do comedy. I read through a variety of authorities on comedy. They all seemed to know exactly what they were talking about, but I did not. It was all vague theory. There was nothing concrete, nothing you could get hold of or sink your teeth into.

They said things like, "Swing a baby toward one of his parents. At the last moment, pull him back. As long as he is unharmed, he will laugh. This is an excellent example of how surprise, alone, can act as a device for humor."

Is surprise an element of humor? The babies I swung toward their parents all cried. The premise did not make sense to me. There are lots of times when we are surprised, yet unharmed, and it is not funny. Try jumping out at someone and saying, "Boo." They are more likely to strike you in fright, or anger, than they are to laugh. Even if I could get this elusive element of surprise to work in a humorous way, how could it be applied in a play or comedy routine?

Still I tucked this little tidbit into my memory bank. Any time I found a magazine article, or another book on theory of humor, my antennae went up. It was not until I shuffled through my old college notes from my directing class at Northwestern University that it all began to fit together. There in my theater notes were three or four specific, concrete rules of physical action. You will find them described in this book. They were not really directed toward creating humor. Their intent was to avoid accidental comic effect in a serious production. Though many years away from being organized into a book, that nucleus grew. Thanks to that, and to working with a couple of very simply yet skillfully constructed Woody Allen and Neil Simon scripts, I really began to understand humor as more than mere theory. It became plain that it could be treated almost as a science. Like "method acting," there were specific techniques that could be organized and systematized in an understandable and practical way. As a result of these techniques, I finally accomplished the ultimate in my High School drama-coaching career.

Finally understanding the techniques of exaggeration, contradiction, and the need to make everything match under the heading of characterization, we produced Shakespeare's *Midsummer Night's Dream.* More than an artistic success, it was a great comic success. I cast a 200 lb, five-foot-seven-inch girl as the fairy queen. In order to emphasize her size, she allowed us to dress her in a white body suit and a red tutu that stood out all around. She dominated every proceeding, just as Shakespeare intended, and did it in a very comic way.

We also modernized the language, being very careful to keep the original rhymes, rhythms and intent. More important, we watched carefully to see where use of the pause could help point up Shakespeare's original thoughts.

With fear and trembling for being so presumptuous as to tinker with the great bard, I told the very strict head of our English department what I was doing. Her disapproval could well mean the kiss of death to our efforts. She came to a rehearsal and was delighted. More important, we had the high school kids "rolling in the aisles" with laughter at Shakespeare.

These techniques can work equally in any kind of performance or situation. Put them to work in your own life. If they can work for me, I know they can work for you. Good luck, and have fun!

R. W. K.

1
IT ONLY HURTS WHEN I DON'T LAUGH

"It must be an elephant. I can feel the trunk."

That's me in the title picture, but actually, it only hurts when I do not laugh at my low vision. Matter of fact, the first step in developing a comic sense is to find things about yourself at which you can laugh…things, which you can satire. It is a truism that there are none so sad as those who cannot laugh at themselves.

At the time of this writing it is politically incorrect to make light of someone's misfortune. But as you will note later, humor is the saving grace. It is the only healing way to survive.

Unfortunately our society has become super sensitive to everything that makes light of almost anything. I am surprised that congress does not pass a law against making fun of congressmen. In fact, I think there was some movement awhile back in that direction.

I am sure this has come about because many humorists have sometimes not used the rules of comedy well. They have gone for "cheap shots," and now even the humor that heals is suspect and taboo. It is something we need to be aware of as we approach the subject of humor.

In the meantime, be assured that all of us are born with a natural ability toward humor. Unfortunately for most of us, the process of growing up causes us to lose it before we really have the chance to discover and develop it. The very essence of humor involves the knack of putting things together in a way that is unexpected, disjointed or inaccurate. Children do this naturally in an effort to sort out what is real, and what is not. On TV, kids see real war on the news. A few moments later they see slapstick cartoons. Until they learn the difference between real and make believe, it is just as funny to them to see an exploded human body fly 25 feet in the air, as it is to see a cartoon figure fall off a cliff. Unless they are aware of the real pain involved in the first instance, it is all just make-believe.

On the other extreme, we adults refuse to allow ourselves to see the humor in situations that involve pain. We fear that others will think we are insensitive, unbalanced or evil for such thoughts. We may even believe that about ourselves, when we have such thoughts. We moderns are not as far from voodoo thinking, as we would like to believe. But mere thinking does not really make it so.

In order to create humor, we must free ourselves from our adult view of the world. We must discard our preconceived ideas that all drinking glasses have bottoms, time moves in linear motion, and the world exists as we have learned to know it. We must approach everything with the fresh innocence of a child. The problem with most of our humor today is it has lost this quality of innocence. On one hand it goes for the cheap shot. On the other hand it has become painfully self-conscious.

A wonderful example of this contrast in thinking is the story about the matronly grandmother who saw her young grandson cutting a fishing worm in two. She was about to scold him for being so cruel. Then she heard him tell the newly divided worm "There, now you have a friend to play with."

Kids are so uninhibited. They say what comes to mind, oblivious as to the reality or consequences. This combination of innocence and searching for reality produces a delightful combination we humans treasure and call creativity. Creativity is what gives us the freedom to put ideas together in new, unexplored ways.

This ability is what enables inventors and artists to do what they do. Humorists are the most prolific users of this creativity. Stand-up comics strive to produce a laugh every 20 to 30 seconds, all as a direct result of the incongruous arrangement of ideas.

Unfortunately, as we grow up, the process of socialization causes us to reject that marvelous seed of creativity within ourselves. We want to be like our elders, so we use them as models. We are frequently ridiculed and belittled by others, and ourselves for our "childish" ideas; so we make ourselves conform to the "norm". In our teen years the pressures become enormous to be exactly like everyone else. Some teens attempt blind rebellion for a while, but most succumb and settle for being just average. Most of us settle for being average because it is just too painful to be ourselves, creatively different from the pack. It is the rare individual indeed that can suffer through the loneliness that comes when you stand up to the pressures of adults, teachers and peers. The ingenious Walt Disney undoubtedly suffered much in his teen years. A bit strange looking and a dreamer, he doodled in the margins of his textbooks and did poorly in school. You can probably think of several more who painfully resisted becoming average, to retain their creativity.

Many of the funniest people you know, got that way through a very painful process of growing up in extremely uncomfortable circumstances. Most of the famous vaudeville comics came out of abject poverty. When you are too poor, too rich, too fat, too thin, too tall or short, or too ugly for your own comfort level, how do you survive?

The easiest, least painful way is to make jokes about it. You do it yourself before others beat you to it. It may be painful to inflict such jokes on yourself, but it is far less painful to do it yourself than to be the brunt of it. Kids are notorious for attacking each other unmercifully for such things. It takes the heat off their own perceived shortcomings, and makes them feel superior. Adults are only a little kinder. They just ignore the obvious and keep silent.

It took me a long time to learn that. I have always had low vision, but it was not severe enough when I was a child to be obvious. Even my parents did not realize it until I was caught in the second grade, cheating on the math flashcards. When the teacher would hold them for the class to call out the answers, I quickly learned to adapt to the norm. Even though I couldn't see the cards, I moved my lips like I knew the answers. I never learned the saving grace of making jokes about my poor vision. I tried to be normal, doing everything like everyone else as nearly as I could, despite the vision problem. Frankly, without any of us realizing it, this made us all very uncomfortable. Co-dependently, none of us talked about it.

Recently, as I began to discover how humor works, I changed my methods. When people greet me with, "Good to see you"; I often respond to my friends with "Good to almost see you, too." We both have a laugh, and feel more comfortable in the relationship.

So how do you make humor work for you? The great abstract painter, Picasso claimed that it took him 60 years to learn to paint like a child. You don't have 60 years? No matter. Picasso did some very creative work even during the early part of those 60 years.

To begin, take it for granted that you already have the same marvelous creative potential you had as a kid. It is only repressed. In addition, remember that anything learned systematically, comes much more quickly and less painfully, then it does being discovered accidentally. True, it is sometimes tedious, tiring, and humorless to the point of pain, to labor over details; but it is far less painful than learning it in the school of hard knocks.

That is what this book is all about. There are ways of developing your innate creativity. There are also many mechanical devices that come in handy in writing and delivery. Some of these basics are dealt with in these pages; but the first, and most important step, is to regain that part of your creativity, which may have been lost in the growing up process.

EXERCISES:

1. LEARNING TO LAUGH AT YOURSELF:

What could someone say about you that would really hurt? What traits do you have that others might find annoying, ridiculous, disturbing or silly? Pick one; think of a way to speak of it in a grossly exaggerated way.

As an example, let us suppose you are sensitive about your weight. Nearly everyone is, even if they are not overweight at all. Suppose you are only slightly overweight. You might humorously comment by exaggeration: "I look like a beached whale in this outfit." If you are really large enough that this is not much of an exaggeration, then say: "I need the Washington DC beltway just to keep my pants up."

Confronting your weight in this manner serves two purposes beyond helping you to build a comic sense. First, if you exaggerate sufficiently, your audience may comment: "Oh, come on. You're not all that big." This will be an ego-booster for you. Secondly, it will help take you out of a state of denial, making it possible for you to openly confront any weight problem you actually may have. When you begin to poke fun at your problems, it can be the first step to solving them.

It is important to exaggerate well beyond the point of actuality. Otherwise it will be realistically painful, instead of unbelievably humorous. Try to come up with a variety of lines. Here are a couple of examples to get you started: "That's not fat. It's muscle that has gone to seed. It is easier to keep my eye on my weight when I have more of it."

2. INCREASING YOUR INNOCENCE LEVEL:

A. When you listen to others, or read, think in terms of taking statements literally. (i.e. "I ran into so-and-so, today.") Looking at the face-value of the line, the natural retort might well be, "Oh, I hope you didn't leave any tire marks on his chest."

B. Think of alternate definitions for the same word. The cartoon at the beginning of this chapter uses this technique. What other kinds of trunks are there? (i.e. tree trunk, railroad trunk line, swimming trunks.) What words sound similar? (i.e. truck—either the one you drive or the one you dance) or turkey (trucky).

C. What confusions arise when phrases or words are said quickly? (i.e. The hymn *"Gladly the Cross I'd Bear"* can come out sounding like *"Gladly, the Cross-eyed Bear."*)

3. INCREASING CURIOSITY:

Examine an object that is strange to you, or a familiar object, examining it as if it were the first time you had ever seen it. Even an empty box with an interesting shape will do. (Remember how kids will play with the boxes and let the toys sit idly by?) How is the object put together? What different uses for the box or other item can you suggest? In the case of a box, it could be a hat, a shoe, baby's cradle or a puppet stage, etc. Magicians will take a drinking glass with no bottom, and find a dozen or more uses for it. Can you?

4. FINDING THE HUMOROUS SIDE OF A SERIOUS SUBJECT:

Check out the news. Find a story that seems to have no saving humor about it at all. See if you can simplify it to its basic elements, to come up with a humorous twist. Below is one example. It employs the simplicity of childlike innocence to create humor. It deals with the capture of the evil dictator, Saddam Hussein, who oppressed an entire nation and murdered many. He lived like a king and had many palaces; but was captured, hiding in a dirty little four by seven foot hole in the ground. At the time, he gave the impression of a ratty-looking guy with bugs in his salt-and-pepper gray hair. The comments are his, as reported on the news. The responses are ours, as we might imagine a child would view things:

Like a chipmunk, he popped his head out of a hole in the ground, and said...

"My name is Saddam Hussein."

"You don't say."

"I am president of Iraq."

"Sure you are. Is the butler out for the day?"

"I would like to negotiate."

"Are we trading baseball cards or marbles?"

Apparently, one soldier on the scene did manage to capture the humor of the situation. His comment, as reported on the news, was: "President Bush sends his regards."

Saturday Night Live could do an entire comedy sketch on it. Like the mind of a child, this cuts to the barest essentials of the situation. Humor is often more obvious when all is stripped away, but the basic outline.

2

PUTTING TWO & TWO FOUR-GETHER

"We vipers are also adders."

PUTTING TWO & TWO FOUR-GETHER

When our youngest boy was four years old, he looked out the car window and said, "Oh, look! There's a three camel bridge!"

Is there any doubt of what type of bridge he saw, even though it is not a completely accurate description? This is the very essence of humor. It springs from innocence and the ability to put things together in a way that makes sense, yet is inaccurate, disjointed, or unexpected.

Let's examine how the disjointed ideas in this example came together. Undoubtedly, the bridge has three humps of super structure. Perhaps we were on our way to the circus or zoo. The point is that animals were bouncing around somewhere in my son's head. Uninhibited with rules of logic, sentence structure and grammar, he was free to allow himself to connect the two ideas.

We laughed with delight at the humorous arrangement of words that made perfect sense—yet were not perfectly sensible.

Looking at the arrangement of ideas strictly from a logical point of view, it was not a bridge for camels. The bridge had absolutely no relationship to camels. Do camels have one or two humps? I don't know. I don't believe I've ever seen a camel with three humps. But then he did not say three humps. He said, "three camels". Nothing really quite fits logically.

The ideas were compressed in a way that was unexpected, disjointed and inaccurate. Yet there was an element of truth that was perfectly clear. Such is the exact nature of a joke.

To make such comic connections, your mind must be totally free to think in such unusual, unconventional patterns. You must be comfortable with being completely different from the norm.

Let us start first with the three camel bridge. Brainstorm what else it might be like. Write down your answers. Here are a few ideas to start with: turtles, McDonald arches, roller coaster, dinosaur skeletons. You should be able to make a list of 20 or more ideas. Be ridiculous: rocks in a lumpy bed, three giant hats, mechanical flowers in the land of the giants. At this point, do not stop to criticize or evaluate anything in the list. That comes later, when you review the list.

Change the size of things: arch supports for a caterpillar, an erector set for the jolly green giant.

No matter what your present creative level, you can raise it considerably with fun games like this. You can even begin to invent the games yourself, and that will increase your creative level.

Check out your front lawn or basement steps. Imagine what life would be like here if you were only 2 inches tall. What if you were 25 feet tall and you accidentally left your car keys in the house? How would you get them? What would you be able to do with them once you found them? These suggestions can be the nucleus for entire comedy skits, stories and routines, as exemplified by the stories in *Alice in Wonderland.*

Pretend you are from a different planet. Imagine that you do not know the language. Try to listen to just the sounds. It has been said that to someone who does not speak it, the English language sounds like a pack of barking dogs. Listen as you pronounce the following with force and firm articulation: who, what, how, when, why, if, just, etc.

Still pretending yourself a stranger from another planet, look at the strange way we humans move, literally falling forward on one foot and then the other. Check out our silly customs and mannerisms. This is the grist from which entire comedy routines are built. The more you play these creativity games, the easier it becomes, and the more ideas it will produce.

Recently I was rolling my suitcase table out to the car. It was a nice day, and I use a dog leash to pull the thing. A passer-by, noticing the pleasantness of the day and the leash, put two and two four-gether and said, "Walking your dog?"

Putting two and two four-gether myself, I responded with, "Yes, he's a boxer!"

It took similar brainstorming techniques to come up with the title of this chapter. I liked the play on words because it illustrated the point exactly, but it seemed a little overly cute for the words to come from my own mouth. Then the idea of the chapter cartoons presented itself, and it all fell into place. The snake could easily say that line, as a natural part of his character.

So much of the "innocence" part of the equation depends on character!

My neighbor was having trouble getting his lawn mower started. He was becoming very frustrated. The 5 year old who lived on the other side of us came over to get in on the action.

He watched for a long time, while my neighbor squatted on the ground, frustrated by a cantankerous lawnmower. Finally, in serious concern, the youngster said, "Mr. Henderson, you really should stop playing with your lawnmower and cut your grass. It sure does need it."

Despite his frustration, or perhaps because of it, Mr. Henderson fell backward off his heels and rolled on the ground in laughter.

The line carried a wonderful feeling of innocence because of the age of the speaker. It was logical that a child might assume Mr. H was just playing. Had I, as an adult, delivered the same line, it would have come across as needling sarcasm.

For me to convey the same idea—that I thought he was just playing around, I would have to use exaggeration to the point of disbelief. I might say, "What a clever way to convince yourself that golf is a better idea. I wonder if I could get my own wife to believe that."

It is a perfect example of comic innocence and disjointed logic. It makes the perfectly innocent assumption that he has things completely under control, and in fact, is just pretending to play around to accomplish his devious plan. The end result is humor. He knows it is an inaccurate, disjointed set of ridiculous ideas; but by some wild stretch of the imagination, there could be some element of truth in my assumption.

Truth and innocence go hand in hand. Once I secretly recorded a family gathering and played it back to the unsuspecting participants. My aunt, shocked from hearing herself for the first time, said, "For goodness sake, I sound like an old biddy."

There was an awkward moment of silence. The truth, on the tape, was abundantly clear. To deny it would have been untruthful. To affirm it would have been painful. Not knowing what to say, I blurted out, "I guess it takes one to know one."

We all had a big laugh and then I re-assured her that we are all our own worst critics, and often judge ourselves more harshly than justified.

The element of truth was still quite plain on the tape, but the comment I had accidentally blurted out was taken as a joke. This, because it seemed to contradict reality. Surely I would not be so cruel as to make such a blunt statement, if I truly believed it. While she might assume the worst, even the phrasing of my comment seemed to indicate that I might not agree with her. It became humor, softening the blow dealt by the truth. This is the nature of humor when delivered with innocence.

Character is all-important as it relates to innocence. Under the umbrella of character, one can even get away with verbal murder. Several years ago, in the sit-com, *All In the Family*, Archie Bunker voiced violent racial slurs, terrible macho insults and continuous narrow-minded bigotry, and we laughed. We laughed because it was all properly exaggerated within his character. We laughed at him instead of hating him, because he was so utterly unaware of his gross bigotry. It was comic, rather than offensive.

Naturally one has to be careful with using humor in this way. Such insults can alienate an audience without your even being aware of it.

I once sat next to a lady who volunteered to help the magician on stage. He performed the bra trick, in which a lady tucks the tied ends of two silk hankies into her bodice. At the count of three, the outer ends of the silk are pulled. She expects another silk hanky to be tied in between, but instead, a bra appears there. The implication, of course, is that it is hers.

In this instance, the lady seemed to be having a really good time laughing it up on stage. She played the part of a wonderful sport, seemingly taking it all in stride, as just good fun.

I was surprised when she came back to her seat. She leaned over to me, a perfect stranger, and said, "I will never again volunteer to help another magician." Even if she, herself, had not felt used, and victimized, undoubtedly there were other ladies in the audience who felt for her.

By contrast, invite a couple of men on stage to hold the ends of the tied hankies. In this case, the magician tells them to concentrate their minds on the hanky he just vanished. "Whatever you have uppermost on your mind will appear in the middle of the tied hankies."

When the bra appears, it will confirm their masculinity. Instead of feeling victimized, they will feel complimented. This puts it all in the realm of just innocent good fun.

What makes the difference? The answer, of course, is a difference in characters. More about characterization later. In the next chapter, we will add specific comedy elements, techniques and devices to the equation.

EXERCISES:

1. Select two or three objects at random, and see if you can figure how to use them together in some comic scenario. The more unrelated the objects are, the better. It will force you to draw ridiculous and exaggerated relationships. For example, At random I will pick a roller window shade, a light bulb, and a pencil. The scenario? Well, The roller blind is to raise up to see how dark it is outside. Why the light bulb? How else do you expect me to see when it's so dark out there? The pencil is because I'm lazy. I won't even make the effort unless I can figure some way to get the lead out.

Alternative scenario: How many light bulbs does it take to change a roller blind? I don't know, but I have a pencil to write down your answer.

I am sure you can do even better. These little examples were drummed up on the spur of the moment. You may use my choice of items, or select others of your own.

2. Think of a person who is extremely irritating to you. Make a list of all of those things that irritate you. Then, mentally pick one trait at a time. In your mind, exaggerate the trait to the point where your irritation changes to laughter. Does the person sniffle, or have a strange cough? Are they continually belittling you or others? Are they picky beyond belief? (For help, you may want to read *Comedy Devices* in the next chapter.) For an example, here, let's select the trait of pickiness. Off the top of my head, my imagination goes to a fussy hen in the barnyard, picking, clucking and squawking as she goes. I would probably give her lines to say, as well.

3

NUTS AND BOLTS MAKE ME SCREWY

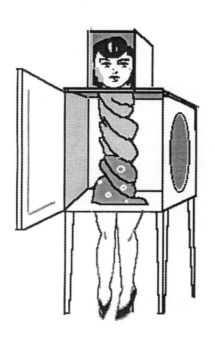

We have divided the various specific techniques of humor, or what we call the nuts and bolts, into two categories. The first, more general, category consists of elements, which are basic to all humor. It includes rules of physical actions, contradiction, exaggeration, distortion, punch line sentence structure, and the pause.

The second category consists of specific devices, which utilize one or more of these elements. Put them together properly and comedy will almost automatically result. We have said before, in referring to these comic techniques and devices, that it is so much easier to handle the nuts and bolts that we often overlook the vitally important girders of innocence, believability and characterization. It is these all-important parts of the structure that tie everything together. Without the super structure, the nuts and bolts become only a string of jokes, losing logic and believability. They become only the utterances of a clumsy fool, who is trying to be cute or clever.

Though it is almost impossible to do so with humor, for the sake of discussion, we shall try to deal with each element separately. There is much overlapping, and sometimes a certain example might just as easily be used to illustrate one rule as another. This is one of the reasons humor is so difficult to pin down. Nevertheless, let us try.

Rules of physical action are many. Here, we shall concentrate on the four that relate the most directly to comedy. The first is a rule, not of comedy, but of standard dramatic action. It bears understanding because its violation produces a comic result.

The rule is: **For an action to be real and believable, it must come with, or immediately preceding, the line it accompanies.**

The biological reason for this rule is that the brain can formulate movement quicker than it can accomplish the complicated task of formulating language. For example, if you were to put your hand on a hot stove, your automatic instincts will cause you to withdraw it instantly. It will take a slight beat later for your brain to formulate the verbalization of an out-cry. It would never be the other way around. You would never cry out in pain, first, and then afterward, remove your hand. The

NUTS AND BOLTS MAKE ME SCREWY 17

action would not match with the word. Try it in front of an audience. (Use an unheated burner, please.) Time it right, and you will get a laugh.

In fact, time it in any way that does not agree with this reality, and you will also get a laugh. Note the description of the slow thinker in the list of comic devices at the end of this chapter. Whenever actions are out of joint in any way with the words, it sets up a contradiction, which is almost always humorous.

The second rule of physical action is a confirmation of the first: **If an action comes after its accompanying words, the result will be comic.**

There is a simple little demonstration you can use to illustrate not only the positive, serious effect of the first rule, and the humorous effect of the second rule, but also the comic effect of rule number three below.

Stand facing a door. Imagine another character on stage, to whom you are talking. Raise your arm firmly, and point to the door. When the arm is in position, wait a beat. Then say, "Go!" Notice how definite and positive, is this combination of words and actions. It makes it a very serious matter, and not comic in the least.

Do it a second time, only this time say the word "Go," at the same time as you raise your arm. Though not as powerfully positive as the first example, again this will come across as a definite, believable order.

Finally, say the line, wait a beat, and then raise your arm. Everything is hopelessly out of joint. There will be no mistaking the comic effect. To carry it further, wait a beat, and then wave your pointed fingers frantically, point and re-point. Walk over to the door and vigorously point some more. The repetition will become funnier and funnier. Such mechanical, overly dramatic actions are frequently the stock-in-trade of comic "mellerdrammers."

The last, repetitious part of the example may just as easily be attributed to exaggeration or repetition; but it is easier to understand and work with it, if we treat it as an example of the third rule of physical action. That is: **Any action extended beyond its logical point will be comic.**

To place this example into a context, let us apply these rules to a magic act. We could also use a play with a story line, or even a real-life situation; but the magic act allows us to center attention on a single character, while still including lines, actions and props as well. Imagine our performer as he waves his wand. If he waves it before or during the time he says the magic word, it will come across as normal and perfectly acceptable dramatic action. But instead, if he says the word before the action it will be comic. Please note that an element of characterization as well as contradiction also creeps in here. It creates comedy by making the magician appear to be uncertain or ineffectual.

Continuing, let us have him illustrate rule number three by having him keep waving the wand. Pause, and then wave it more frantically. Use more exaggerated movements. Even move both hands together as if illustrating the curvaceous form of a lovely lady. Nothing seems to work. Finally, he points the wand directly at the object, which he intends to influence. A flash of fire appears at the end of the wand, and the object finally reacts. This grand climax will cause the audience to applaud, not only for the magic, but also for the magician's ability to make it happen, despite what appears to be overwhelming odds against it. In the process the audience will appreciate him for having given them a good laugh as well.

Of course, we do not need to limit ourselves only to actions, coupled to just a word or two. We did this strictly to illustrate the point. With words alone, we can also illustrate rule number 3. Take the line, "My father and I did the same act together, for many years after his death." Something is left out. The thought continues beyond its logical point. Naturally, the comic impact of this line can be enhanced through use of the pause just after the word "together". More about the pause in the next chapter.

The fourth rule of physical action is: **If the line and action are directly contradictory, the audience will believe the action rather than the word.**

That is because people often lie; perhaps do not really know the truth; change their minds; or refuse to verbally reveal what they actually think. Thus the expression, "actions speak louder than words."

This sort of contradiction is always a useful tool of comedy. Whenever a direct contradiction becomes obvious, it causes laughter. As an example of this rule, let us place a character in the center of a room. Obstinately, he firmly asserts that he absolutely will not sit on the sofa, as directed. Then after considering for a moment, he goes directly to the sofa and sits. The result is laughter. Virtually every example we have used so far has had some element of contradiction embedded somewhere within it, but contradiction is often the basic element.

In my own comedy ring routine, the performer claims that he will accomplish a certain thing. Then something else happens, instead. Holding up three rings that are linked, he tries, vigorously, to unlink the left ring from the center ring. Instead, the right ring falls off. This kind of thing happens throughout the entire routine.

Try dressing in a formal tuxedo or set of tails and top hat. Then add a very obvious pair of old high top tennis shoes to the costume, and you will create humor.

Make fantastic claims about what miracles you can perform, and then trip over your own feet.

Kole and Company do an entire act this way. They drive audiences wild with laughter. He vanishes gloves, only to have them accidentally revealed a moment later, hanging from his backside. He tries to hypnotize his lady assistant in order to saw her in half. Instead, his male assistant, who is standing behind to catch the lady, falls flat on his face in a trance. It goes on and on. There are many contradictions within the act, but the major contradiction lies in the fact that impresario master magician Kole, moves about the stage in great dignity, never quite aware of the mayhem he is creating around him.

Now, let us integrate the basic elements of humor into specific comedy devices. There is a neat little book, currently out of print, called *Comedy Techniques for Entertainers*. The author, Bruce "Charlie" Johnson, does an excellent job of cataloging many of the standard comic devices that have been developed throughout the years. By permission, we include the bulk of his list, intermingling our own explanations and illustrations with his. See if you can identify the various basic comic element (such as contradiction, exaggeration, distortion, rules of physical action and the like) involved in each device. You will also note that each device works better when you assume that a certain specific character is involved. This adds greatly to the believability factor.

For further information and other books by this author, write:

Charlie's Creative Comedy
P. O. Box 82165,
Kenmore WA 98028-0165
www.Charliethejugglingclown.com.

SPECIFIC COMEDY DEVICES

SLOW THINKER: The title, itself, suggests the technique. Either verbally, or otherwise, the character is slow on the up-take. He may delay his reaction to pain for a few seconds, while the audience waits in anticipated delight for him to react. Buster Keaton and Stan Laurel perfected this device. They used all sorts of variations based on the first two rules of physical action, as explained earlier in this chapter. In their facial expressions, you can see the cogs grind in their heads.

Another type of slow thinker is the otherwise normal acting individual who does a double take. He is so pre-occupied with other things that it takes about five seconds for some important event to sink in. He keeps on with his other activity and then stops abruptly, in midstream, to react.

In movie cartoons, a character may run off the edge of a cliff, but not fall, until he realizes that he is in danger. Only when he tries to retreat, does he fall.

REPETITION: Identical repetition is funny in and of itself, or as a means of setting up a gag. Some say that three times is the limit. Others say that seven is the magic number. Trial and error will tell. When the laughter starts to diminish after a repetition, you have taken it one step too far. Next time you will know better.

As an example, I have a pet rope, which does imitations: a white line going down the highway; a white line going up the highway; a drunk man looking at a white line going down the highway (double the rope); and a blind man looking at a white line going down the highway (hold up nothing). Up to this point, each repetition becomes funnier. To take it any further begins to lose impact.

DELAYED ANTICIPATED ACTION: Repetition is often used to set up this gag. The audience, through continued repetition, begins to expect a certain thing will happen. When it does not, it produces a laugh. Then, when the thing actually does happen later, it produces another laugh.

In *The Quiz Show* episode of *I Love Lucy*, Lucy goes on a game show. She is asked to sing *My Bonnie Lies Over the Ocean*. Every time she mentions anything associated with water, the MC squirts her with a seltzer bottle. (Repetitions) Following the song, she grabs a spare bottle from the table to squirt the M.C.; but it is rigged to shoot backwards so she squirts herself. (Variations) Later the show's cast is relaxing backstage, and the M.C. is mixing drinks. He picks up a seltzer bottle, but it is the rigged one, so he gets squirted, too. (Reversal)

REVERSAL: The three types are situation, character and role. Stories where the worm turns are examples of the situation device. The puny little weakling changes his ways to beat the bully.

In character reversals, the same character exhibits contradictory traits. For example, a hulking football player turns into a blubbering baby when someone stands up to him.

Role reversal involves a character taking on the role of another. Vainly, a husband tries to do the housework, and tend the squalling children; while the housewife finds she is out of her element, when she attends the executive board meeting.

IMPERSONATION: A character tries to convince others that he is someone else. Example: a clown dons a set of formal tails and steps to a grand piano. By using a hidden recording and pantomiming the actions, he manages to surprise the audience with a perfect performance—until the recording skips a groove, causing the illusion to fall apart.

MISTAKEN IDENTITY: One or more people, meeting for the first time, may believe the other to be someone else. A prim matron may believe that the book salesman at the door is the new minister of her church, whom she has never met. The salesman, getting the wrong address, may believe the lady is interested in x-rated materials. The confusions in conversation that follow can be ripe with humor.

IMAGINED PREDICAMENT: A character creates the situation, which is totally in his imagination. For instance, he reads the wrong medical report and believes that he has some serious illness. His efforts at coping take on a comic bent.

Alternatively, a character daydreams, imagining that, instead of being a klutz, he is a dashing hero. In his imagination his klutzy qualities get him in trouble, but he miraculously overcomes them with his imagined heroic prowess. *The Secret Life of Walter Mitty* is an excellent example.

SPOONERISM: Named after William Spooner, who was prone to these. Sections of two side-by-side words are accidentally transposed. A famous radio announcer accidentally exhorted his listeners with "Ladies and Gentlemen, the President of the United States, "Hoobert Heaver." Another radio announcer embarrassed himself by introducing a popular alcoholic drink as "Bupert's Reer."

MALAPROP: Using the wrong word in a sentence. It sounds similar to the proper word, but is completely wrong in meaning. The name of this device is taken from the name of a character in Sheridan's play, *The Rivals.* Mrs. Malaprop was prone to its use. There are two malaprops in the following sentence: "My dear Watson, the solution to the crime was alimentary. It was a mere matter of logical seduction."

THE PUN: This is a play on words. Words that sound alike, but may have different meanings make excellent puns.

Q: What did the buffalo say to her son when he went off to school?
A: Bye, son. (Bison)

The cartoon sub-title, at the beginning of chapter two, also relies on the pun for its humor.

DOUBLE ENTENDRE: These are statements that can be taken more than one way. Often, though not always, one meaning has sexual overtones. Here is an example that does not: "When he was accidentally hit in the head, he was taken to the hospital. The X-rays of his head showed nothing."

WORD DISTORTION: As the name implies, this involves the use of the proper word, but mispronouncing it, or inserting additional syllables to distort it. "The sportscaster gave a very clear description of the boxing match."

"We are proud that this newspaper has not made a typograsphical error in sex years."

CREATING A NEW WORD: "You need to be a millionaire to afford living in those new downtown lofts. They call them condomaximums." Another example is found in the title of the previous chapter: *Putting Two and Two Four-gether.*

ALLITERATION: A series of words having similar sounds. Tongue twisters are simple examples. Extended alliteration can be hilarious as in this excerpt from a *Fibber McGee & Molly* show:

Fibber: I had a trading post in pygmy country. That's how the expression this little pigmy went to market got started.

Bigam: You must have been a splendid companion on a long trek.

Fibber: That's what everyone used to say. I was really a card on a long trek. Card Trek McGee they called me. Card Trek McGee, the cleverest Khaki clad kid who ever kept a camp in the cruel climate of the carbon continent calmly collecting creeping cobras to classify and catalogue for keen eyed collectors, casually clicking cameras at carnivorous cats, continually convulsed at the cute conversational come backs of cackling cockatoos, and concentrating on carving a career as the King Kong of the Congo from the Cape of Good Hope's cloudy dunes to carefree Cairo and the Cameroon's.

(This entire speech, beginning with "Card Trek McGee, the cleverest…" was given on one breath in rapid fire. The completion of its climax created tumultuous cheering.)

For a subtler example, check out the Gilbert and Sullivan operettas. Often the patter songs are saturated with alliteration, especially when each word and syllable is pronounced crisply and precisely. It creates a delightful effect. Here is just one sample. It uses the *m, n, d,* and *t* sounds in a delightfully complex arrangement. (The word "vegetable" is pronounced with four syllables, and the words "mineral" and "general" are each pronounced with three syllables.) "In fact in matters animal, vegetable and mineral, I am the very model of a modern major general."

NON-SEQUITURS: When certain segments of thought do not agree, or certain thought segments are left out, it causes the audience to do a double take. Yogi Berra is famous for these.

"When you come to a fork in the road, take it."

"Tell me, sir, do your ideas come first; or do you write first, and then get your ideas?"

TWISTED LOGIC: Comic characters don't do things to be funny, but for funny reasons. They have their own way of thinking that is different from others. In one episode of the *Burns & Allen Show,* George saw Gracie putting salt into the peppershaker, and pepper into the saltshaker. When he asked Gracie why, she said, "Well, people are always picking up the wrong one, and this way when they're wrong they're right."

SELF-DEPRECATION: The entertainer allows some of the jokes to be at his own expense. At the beginning of the first chapter, we made quite a point of the importance of making light of one's own shortcomings. Be careful not to carry it too far. Your character needs some redeeming qualities to make him appealing to the audience.

ANCIENT-MODERN: Different eras of history are mixed to provide a comic effect. The play, *Skin of Our Teeth,* by Thornton Wilder, has the maid vacuuming the carpet, while outside, the dinosaurs are playing. *The Flintstones* offers a modern example.

RECIPROCAL DESTRUCTION: One character accidentally, or deliberately, damages property of another. The injured party surveys the damage, usually calmly, and then deliberately returns damage to the other. This seesaw destruction continues until all is a shambles. For the greatest humor, it is often done in a quite calm and deliberate manner.

PUT DOWN & RETORT: This is a verbal version of reciprocal destruction. An insult is hurled, and the alternate character responds with a greater insult. This usually continues until one or the other runs out of ammunition, and concludes by sputtering out some feeble response such as, "So's your old man."

GETTING IT ALL WRONG: One character clearly explains a situation or tells a joke to the second character. When the second character tries to repeat the story, he gets it all wrong. The most famous example is the Abbott and Costello routine, "*Who's on First Base?*"

Here is another example: A first character comments, "It must be raining cats and dogs outside. I just stepped in a poodle."

The second character tries to repeat the joke to a third party by saying, "It must be raining cats and dogs outside. I just stepped in a puddle."

LITERAL MEANING: The literal interpretation of a phrase, especially an old saying, is useful in comedy. It can be used to point up the humor of what we all say and don't pay attention to, or to show a character's stupidity.

On *The Charlie McCarthy Show,* ventriloquist Edgar Bergen advised Mortimer Snerd to keep his shoulder to the wheel. Mortimer replied, "Which shoulder? What wheel?"

SATIRE: This is comedy used to expose follies and abused. *Gulliver's Travels* and *Alice in Wonderland* are famous satires on the politics of their times. Will Rogers is famous for his humor in this direction.

EXAGGERATION: This is a basic element in most humor, but it may also be used as a specific device, such as: "My hotel room is so small that...

The mice were hunchbacked."

NUTS AND BOLTS MAKE ME SCREWY 27

"I had to go outside to change my mind."

UNDERSTATEMENT: This is the opposite of exaggeration. It is associated with the British sense of humor. It deflates the seriousness and importance of an event. The response to a report that somebody was stepped on by an elephant might be "I do declare. That might hurt a bit."

In another example, a character might exit the stage, followed by a yell, and extended crashing and thumping sounds, only to return with the report "I fell down." Care must be taken to make sure the audience knows you are kidding, and not just being unsympathetic.

To this very extensive list of comic techniques, as compiled by Mr. Johnson, I would like to add a couple of comic techniques of my own:

EXPRESSING THE OBVIOUS: Need I say more? The name of this technique, itself, provides its own definition. So let us go directly to an example. This one is taken from one of my own routines.

"I would now like to present the most famous magical mystery in the world. Everyone talks about it, but virtually no one, today, has ever seen it. I refer to the production of a white rabbit from a borrowed top hat. Does someone have a top hat I could borrow? So there you are. That is probably why you never see that trick any more."

This particular example provides a three-laugh sequence. The request to borrow a top hat from someone in an audience of today is totally ridiculous. It is obvious that no one will have such. To ask, produces a big laugh. The next line also goes without saying. If no one has a hat to borrow, then, obviously, the trick cannot be done. It provides a smaller, secondary laugh. Then, if the last line is delivered with gusto, as if suddenly becoming aware of the fact, it gets a laugh almost as big as the first line. The word "probably" has a lot to do with this. It understates the obvious. The word "undoubtedly" would not work as well.

EXTENDING THE THOUGHT: With this technique, one finishes a thought completely. Then, as an after thought, adds to it in a way, which contradicts it, or amplifies it in some comic way.

"I was born in a little log cabin, which I helped my father build."

The contradiction is humorous; but easily missed, unless you break it into two separate sentences, using an obvious pause between the two.

"I was born in a little log cabin." Then, after a lengthy pause for puzzled consideration, add, "Which I helped my father build."

Mark Twain often used this technique. If one merely reads casually through his work, it is easy to miss a good deal of the humor. Hal Holbrook brought out the humor orally, in his interpretation of Mark Twain. I am sure I miss-quote the line somewhat, but the line below is an excellent example of Twain's usage.

"In Nevada City there was a brothel at every corner, and three taverns in between. It was no place for a Presbyterian. (Expressing the obvious) And I did not remain one for long."

In the writing, I am sure that Twain used only a comma after the word "Presbyterian" and no capital on the word "and" that follows. In the reading, Holbrook uses a definite period to end the thought. Then, after a lengthy pause, adds the final phrase. By doing so, he gets two laughs, instead of just one.

This leads us directly into the consideration of timing and the pause; and the vital importance of both to the creation of really big laughs.

4
IT'S THE PAUSE THAT IMPRESSES!

◆

—apologies to Coke

"Some light refreshment? Well, maybe just a swallow."

30   GET MORE LAUGHS FROM YOUR LAUGHS

It matters not whether you do stand-up comedy, magic, ventriloquism, silent or patter, every act or story will have a sense of rhythm to it. Allowed to happen unconsciously, it is likely to produce either a dull and plodding movement, or one that is too fast for the audience to follow. The only other possibility is a movement that is uneven, irregular, and unsettling to the point of destroying audience appreciation via confusion.

You must develop your rhythm (sometimes called timing) consciously. Only in that way can it produce a comfortable flow to the act. Then this flow can be interrupted from time to time, with greater or longer pauses, for comic effect. This pausing for comic effect is what can be more aptly called timing. Most inexperienced performers need to start this process consciously. Later it often becomes automatic.

Unfortunately, a good sense of comedy timing can be developed fully, only through experience in front of an audience; but there are certain things you can do in advance to help the process.

There is no better place to start than with the all-important, yet relatively elementary, rules related to use of the pause. Though these pauses can be rather mechanically placed, still, comedy is never quite that simple. We cannot discuss the pause without relating it to matters of dual reality, punch line sentence structure, characterization, and the use of exaggeration.

First, let us look at the rules for the pause. There are only two. You must pause just before the punch line, and again just after. The first pause alerts the audience that something significant is coming. The second pause allows them time to react. If the first pause is not located in just the right spot, or is not extremely positive and definite, the first pause simply will not alert the audience sufficiently for them to "get it". The pause that comes afterward must be long enough to allow the audience time to react. If it is not long enough, they will not react for fear of missing something. If it is too long, they will resent you for waiting on them, expecting them to laugh.

IT'S THE PAUSE THAT IMPRESSES! 31

These are your own secret reasons for pausing. The audience must be given other reasons. If they ever suspect that you are deliberately pausing, trying to make them laugh, they will resent it and refuse to laugh. You want them to receive these alert and courtesy signals without them even being aware that you are sending them.

That means you must give the audience some other reason they will accept as the "real" reason you are pausing. You have your technical reasons. The audience must be given logical reasons. I call this "dual reality". Dual reality simply means you must send unmistakable signals that this is supposed to be a joke. You do this at the same time you are sending contradictory signals that it is real.

This is not as complicated as it sounds. To understand it fully, let us first deal with the psychological reasons why this is so difficult for a beginner. A beginner often sees these pause requirements only as mechanical devices, unrelated to motivation. The pause just before the funny part often needs to come at a spot where you would normally never pause. It may even come right in the middle of the thought.

Let us create an example. Take a look at the line, "This is a very difficult trick if you don't know how to do it."

There is a little disjointed quality to the statement, but certainly nothing sufficient to make an audience laugh. If someone did see the humor and wanted to laugh, he probably would not do so for fear of offending the speaker, or embarrassing himself. It might have been only an accidental misstatement. The audience is not sure whether to laugh or not.

Now let us insert the pauses so that it makes comic sense: "This is a very difficult trick. (Pause) Especially if you don't know how to do it!" (Pause)

As you can see, we have placed a period after the word "trick" and added a word after the period. The period requires a longer pause, and should be more than fully executed. The added word helps to execute the pause, and also allows time for actions to fill the void. Such actions can also be helpful in the second pause, after the punch. These kinds of pauses can be awkward for both you and your audience—you for fear they will not laugh, and they for believing that you are just trying to be funny.

Actions are most helpful in making the pausing believable and natural. During the first pause you might go to your pocket to bring out a set of instructions. Then say the second half of the line as you start to read. During the second pause, you can continue to read until the audience begins to react. If they do not, no one, except you, will be the wiser. You are "home-free" whether they laugh or not. Throw the instructions aside, and shrug your shoulders. Even at this late point, it is possible that your actions, alone, may produce a laugh.

This second pause, the one after the punch, is usually the most difficult for the inexperienced performer to make. It is an agony, waiting and praying for them to laugh. You can see how providing an "excuse" for this pause is most helpful.

In order to make these pauses work for him, the famous George Burns would often take a puff on a cigar. Apparently he just needed a drag. Really he was allowing time for the meaning to sink in.

As you study this chapter, try to relate it to what you see in comedy presentations. Situation comedy shows are excellent to watch when studying how to provide audience-reasons for the pause. Naturally there are both good and poor sit-coms. Be sure to pick the ones that have won awards. Do not depend on audience ratings to be the best judge of what is good.

Since there is a plot structure, it is easier for the writers and performers to come up with logical motivation for these "created" pauses. In observing sitcoms, however, the problem is that when they are done well, you will not notice the pauses as easily. They come so naturally that they are hard to detect. In studying a plotted comedy structure, also be aware that sometimes just shifting from one character to another often substitutes for the first of the two pauses. First, a short straight-line is delivered by one character, followed by a quip from the

IT'S THE PAUSE THAT IMPRESSES! 33

second. The shift in characters often serves the same purpose as the pause, in alerting the audience.

Perhaps the easiest source to work with, in studying the pause, and learning how to provide motivation, can be found in the Victor Borge videotapes. These, and works of other famous comics, can be ordered from many on-line bookstores. The Borge tapes are also a good source for study of contradiction, exaggeration, and use of props for comic effect. As a Danish concert pianist, his problems with the language allows for logical pauses, as he struggles to find the right word.

What are some of the things you can do to make the pausing believable? Here are just a few ideas:

Could be that you need to deal with a prop. Or is a lock of hair falling in your face and does it need a moment to push it up? Are your glasses sliding down?

Perhaps you can convey the idea that you have lost your train of thought and are thinking of what to say next. Maybe you are concerned, wondering if you just said that the right way. In extremely exaggerated pausing, you might even walk a step after delivering a line. Then stop a moment in your tracks and hit your forehead in shock over the stupid thing you just said.

Whatever the reason you might give to the audience to believe, your real reason is that the pauses must be there for them to get it.

Another important aid to easier use of the pause, lies in careful punch line sentence structure. Sometimes the pause can come automatically if the sentence is worded right. For outstanding examples of excellent punch line sentence structure, get a copy of one of Neil Simon's plays. He has a way of wording comedy lines so that even an amateur production can get good laughs.

In the meantime, take a look at the cartoon at the beginning of this chapter. Since the line is not to be delivered orally, the pauses must be built into the sentence structure. The reader must be able to hear the pauses in his own head.

34 GET MORE LAUGHS FROM YOUR LAUGHS

The first pause is located at the question mark, just before the punch line. A question always requires a longer pause, allowing time for an expected answer. In the case of this cartoon, the speaker would normally extend the pause a bit, by the need to consider his own answer.

In the case of a print cartoon like this, there is no way to actually put a pause after the punch, but it still must be worded in a way so as to imply a pause immediately after. There is a rule for this particular wording. It goes like this: The punch line must always be worded so that the significant word or phrase comes at the very end.

Originally I had the punch line worded: "Well, maybe a swallow will do." "Swallow" is the punch word. By adding the extra words, the line talks past the punch, and steps on the laugh.

Finally, we must consider how long to make the pauses. Certainly they must be exaggerated sufficiently in length for the comedy to come across, but how far can you go before it becomes corny or overbearing? You decide how long by relating the degree of exaggeration of the pause, to the degree of exaggeration found in the character you present.

The next logical question is how much can you exaggerate the character? That is a problem for the next chapter.

Suffice it to say, here, that you will probably not exaggerate enough. It is scary to make a fool of yourself, so you will likely make your exaggeration too feeble, out of fear. Make the exaggeration seem logical, and the sky is the limit. The audience will sit breathless, in anticipation. The late Jack Benny has been called the all-time master of the pause. He could stand, silent, just looking at the audience; and get a laugh.

During one of his shows he played the victim of a hold-up.

"Your money or your life!" ordered the gunman.

Now, realize that Benny had built his character as an exaggeratedly tight-fisted miser. When this threat was made, he stood absolutely silent. He thought for a long time about that one. In anticipation, the audience began to titter. The order came again.

IT'S THE PAUSE THAT IMPRESSES! 35

"Well, hurry up. What's it gonna be? Your MONEY or your LIFE!?"

In deep anguish the answer finally came: "I'm thinking! I'm thinking!"

The audience reaction was deafening. It was probably the longest comic pause in history. Certainly it was very exaggerated in length, but it did not seem so because it was solidly grounded in the logic of character.

EXERCISES: Try your hand at arranging a comedy line so that the punch is at the end, allowing for a laugh immediately following. Also decide where to put an "alert" pause to come just before the punch. Each problem below is designed to illustrate a particular rule of punch line sentence structure.

1. When I was at the top of the World Trade Center, I was aware of being pretty high. Can you think of any place where you might have been higher?

Poorly worded punch line: "When I get drunk, I'm pretty high."

Better wording: "I'm pretty high when I get drunk."

This correctly puts the humorous twist of thought at the end of the line, but is still not good. The word "drunk" is too concrete. By explaining too much, it does not leave anything to the imagination of the audience. There should be just enough information given to let your audience draw its own conclusion.

Preferred wording: "I got pretty high last New Year's Eve."

2. There are several playing cards on the table. The magician turns to a volunteer and says: "Take your time to think it over carefully, but sometime this evening I would like you to pick one of these cards."

Better wording, but not the best: "I would like you to think it over carefully and pick one of these cards." (Pause) "Sometime this evening."

36   GET MORE LAUGHS FROM YOUR LAUGHS

This succeeds in putting the humorous part of the line in its proper place, but does not insure a pause before the last phrase. It leaves the timing at the mercy of the volunteer, who may select the card too quickly.

Preferred wording: "In a moment I would like you to pick one of these cards, but please think it over very carefully." (Pause) "Some time this evening, please."

This phrasing leaves the volunteer waiting for further instruction as to when she should point out her choice. This way, the pause is under control of the performer. He may finish the sentence according to his own best judgment of timing.

3. In the following one-liners, locate the best spot to place the "alert" pause, which comes before the punch. Several of these one-liners are also too wordy. Too many words confuse the audience and also come across as if attempting to explain the point. Tain't funny if your audience senses you are setting them up or explaining the point. Can you sharpen these up, as well as locating the best spot for the pause?

A. "I just received this letter from a loan company. Now you can borrow enough money to get completely out of debt."

Place the pause just after the word "money." Think of it as only a place to take a quick breath.

B. "I'll be back here again next winter. I know, because I overheard the owner say that it will be a cold day when I have this guy back again."

Preferred wording: "I'll be back here next winter. I just heard the owner say it." (Pause) "He said 'It will be a cold day when I have that guy back again.'"

Shifting from narration to a direct quote requires a bit of a pause. Breaking the quote into a separate sentence also helps. Thus, the pause is built in. This revision also eliminates some excess wording. The simpler you can keep it, the more likely you are to get the point across without sounding like you are explaining.

IT'S THE PAUSE THAT IMPRESSES! 37

C. "Before I was a performer, I was a taste tester for the Sunsweet Prune Company. I worked one day on, and three off. I must say that it always kept me on the go."

Preferred wording: "Before I was a performer, I was a taste tester for the Sunsweet Prune Company. I must say that..." (Pause, and then slow down) "...it always kept me on the go." (Pause) "I worked one day on, and three days off." (Pause)

You might possibly pause just before the word "go", but this may be a little heavy-handed, especially with material that may be somewhat offensive to certain people. Better pause early and slow down, as if suddenly realizing what you are accidentally saying. The sentence about "time off" is another thought, and deserves its own laugh. Located in the middle of things, it not only gets lost, but also confuses the thought flow.

D. "I'm going to attempt to do this next feat without a net. Did you hear me? Without a net! Annette couldn't be here tonight."

Preferred wording: "I'm going to attempt to do this next feat without a net. Absolutely without a net!" (Pause) "Annette couldn't be here tonight."

The one sentence was removed because it is totally unnecessary to the joke, slows things down, and belligerently browbeats the audience. Simply by saying the second sentence with emphasis gets the point across, and automatically allows for a pause just before the punch line. Be sure you make the pause after the exclamation point a longer pause than the one after the first sentence. The punch on this one may take a little extra time for them to catch it. Have sufficient action you can do, so that it will not appear that you are waiting for the laugh to happen.

4. An upper GI involves a doctor using tools through the mouth to examine the upper intestine. A lower GI involves a similar examination through the colon. For the purposes of this example, both procedures are to be done at the same time. Can you think of a humorous way to ask in which order the procedures will be done?

YOUR COMMENT:

There are several possible good ones. The one we like best is: "Do you do the upper GI first, or wash the tools in between?" Catching the mood of the moment, my doctor replied, "We do if we like the patient."

5
PRESS SHIFT F5 FOR CHARACTER ALIGNMENT

Charlie Chaplin, speaking about his start in movies said, "Little as I knew about movies, I knew that nothing transcended personality."

Neal Simon has said, "It's not just the situation, it has to be the character in the situation."

According to Goodman Ace, "It is more important to develop a situation and to build up a character then to go for big belly laughs. I'll throw away a sure-fire joke anytime rather than sacrifice character. Once you develop a good recognizable character, you get yuks even with soft lines."

Entertainers at amusement parks are sometimes followed around by children who watch show after show. Gags do not have enough appeal to cause the children to do this. They do it because they feel the character is a friend.

All too often, performers develop a vague generic character, hiding behind such things as one-liners, comic devices (see Chapter 3), props and general techniques that produce laughs for the moment, but do not develop loyalty or identification with the performer.

When the performer does not put his trust in personality, he becomes like a clown who hides behind his make-up. The result is that most stand-up comics sound like they came from the same cookie cutter. There is nothing to make them stand out from the crowd. It is character, not the material, with which others can identify.

This means that it is beside the point to ask how much you can exaggerate without being corny or over-bearing. So long as all is exaggerated in complete agreement with the character, and all to the same degree, the sky is the limit—with two very important exceptions:

First, the character must be likeable. He can even be obnoxious and we will still like him, so long as you give him an Achilles heel. That is to say, give him a couple of weaknesses or foibles that make him human.

Secondly, make the exaggeration only great enough for them to get the point that it is a spoof, and not the real thing. The audience must feel that they have recognized, on their own, that it is a spoof. To

PRESS SHIFT F5 FOR CHARACTER ALIGNMENT

repeat the old adage one more time, "if you have to explain it (make it obvious), it just ain't funny."

It is easier to see all of this if we look first at exaggeration, as it exists in "real life" drama. In the movies we see totally implausible, unrealistic and grossly exaggerated auto chases between cops and robbers. We accept them as real. We "believe" in Santa Claus and Mickey Mouse. From a strictly logical point of view, the characters of Rambo and Superman are grossly exaggerated from the norm. Can you imagine yourself, walking along the street, and having a man dressed in blue underwear and a red bed sheet, swoop out of the sky to greet you? We believe and accept these exaggerations because they all fit together in a logical and unified way. There is no need to go into a technically detailed explanation as to why Superman flies, or how Mickey Mouse talks. If explanation is used at all, it is only just barely enough to make the characters plausible.

Comedy works pretty much the same way. Comic contradiction, timing including the pause, vocal expression, costuming, various traits such as brashness or timidity (the list could go on and on), all must be exaggerated to the same degree, as is the exaggeration of the character, himself.

If everything is unified around the character, the picture will be logical and believable, even though it is out of joint with reality. It is unevenness of exaggeration that comes off sounding overdone and corny.

With comedy, as with drama, everything must fit together perfectly. But with comedy it must fit together just barely, and with a slight bit of a kink here and there. The audience must see the logic in what the character is about. At the same time, the audience must also see where his mind "jumped the trolley". It must be perfectly sensible nonsense. Refer back to chapter two and the example of the three camel bridge.

Many years ago, Gracie Allen, of the famous Burns and Allen team, provided a classic example of this. She was stirring cake batter when she had to free her hands for another activity. She handed the bowl and spoon to a friend, who started stirring in the opposite direction. Quickly she took it back, exclaiming, "Oh, no! Not that way. You'll unwind it!"

Like timing, characterization will develop with or without planning. Allowed to develop without conscious thought, you are apt to produce an uneven effect. This, at the very least, will be confusing to an audience. You may also end up producing a characterization that is abrasive and annoying. We do not laugh at characters we do not like, except in ridicule.

The best way to build a character is to do it consciously. The easiest way to understand how to build that character is to look at the way others have done it.

It is difficult to find examples that are familiar to all, so I have selected two of long-standing fame, hoping that enough have seen them to draw the examples. If not, the two are sufficiently well known that audio or video recordings of their work can be found. If you can locate recordings of both their earlier and later works, the comparison in timing and use of the pause is remarkable. I have an early 78 rpm recording of Jack Benny doing several of his most famous routines, before his character had fully matured. On these early recordings, he merely delivers the lines as written. They sound old and hackneyed. In later recordings, when he uses the pausing as dictated by a more fully developed character, the same sketches sound fresh, spontaneous and alive. They are no longer just comic lines. They become part of a precise character. I tire easily of listening to the first. I never tire of listening to the later sketches, even though they are the same lines, and I have heard them often.

Now, let us take that brief look at a couple of classic comedy characters, and compare the degree of exaggeration, as it exists between the two:

BOB HOPE

He uses mild or "realistic" character traits. They are so slightly exaggerated that they seem like the norm. We do not think of him as a comically devised character at all. Instead, we think of Bob Hope as being "just that type of guy." He seems normal, but just a little quirky. To say this, glosses over the clever way the character is constructed. The traits he projects are ingeniously selected to make us laugh.

At first we see a bragging, somewhat arrogant show-off. This is not a character that would gain our sympathy, but we are made aware that these traits merely cover up the underlying traits of timidity and insecurity. This provides both an Achilles heel, and a major comic contradiction.

His reasons for the pause will need to center around this contradiction. He tells a joke with boldness, and then deliberately waits for a laugh. (Ordinarily, this is a comic no-no). When the laugh does not come, he reacts with helpless, agonized hurt, waiting for the laugh. Since he is an obnoxious braggart unveiled, we do laugh—not at the joke, but at him, and his discomfort. We delight in seeing him get his just desserts. If he were a sympathetic character to begin with, and really got into trouble, we would not laugh for fear of offending him and embarrassing ourselves.

With such slight distortion of reality, the timing and exaggeration is very difficult to do. It is like using delicate strokes to paint a tiny flower on a piece of china, versus making broad swipes with a brush to paint a billboard. When the exaggeration is slight, each stroke must be just barely distorted enough from the norm for us to get the point. The margin for error is quite narrow.

JACK BENNY

In the early days of radio, many assumed that Benny's skinflint character was no more of an exaggeration than that of Bob Hope's braggart. Though Benny's character was drawn with broad "billboard" strokes, many still believed him to be truly stingy. He has unified the elements of comedy so well that, even though the tight-fisted character was grossly exaggerated, it was still too believable for many. Enough refused to tune-in to the radio show that it became necessary for Benny to leak the fact that, in real life, he was actually very generous. At the same time, he also made his already broad exaggeration even broader, in order as to make it more obvious that all was merely a spoof. Is there any man on earth so tight-fisted as to have his money buried in a private vault; guarded by an alligator; a moat; a siren; and a guard, so isolated and ancient, that he does not know whether or not Hoover was re-elected?

In later years, long after the vain, tight-fisted character was well established as a spoof, he did numerous programs to help local philharmonic orchestras to raise money. A friend of mine related this instance to me:

"We took three of our best violinists to the station to welcome Mr. Benny. When he arrived, the trio greeted him with the strains of his familiar theme song, *Love in Bloom*. Benny stopped them with a wave of his hand. "That is not the way to play it," he cautioned.

"Taking one of the violins, he screeched out his off-key version. Then he handed the instrument back, tipped his hat, and passed it around through the gathering crowd for contributions."

He played this tightwad character at every chance he got. Is there any doubt why his exaggeration had to be gross for his audience to "get it?"

Benny was also known as the master of the pause. He could wait almost endlessly, just staring at his audience, in hurt anger when his vain character was insulted. In complete silence, without speaking a single word, he got laughs. His pauses could be so broad because they agreed with all other elements of his grossly exaggerated character. Yet, because of his skill, the perception of many was that this was "normal." You will find some comedians who have gone even farther in their exaggeration, but the good ones always make sure that everything they do is unified under the umbrella of character.

PRESS SHIFT F5 FOR CHARACTER ALIGNMENT   45

How do you go about building your own comic character? The most direct way, and probably the way that will produce the easiest character to maintain, is to develop someone that is close to your own personality.

First, analyze what is a little ridiculous about yourself, or by some exaggeration, can be made to look ridiculous. In other words, you must be willing to poke fun at yourself. This may help, later, in providing your character with an Achilles heel. Naturally, this is not a comfortable thing to do. It may even be painful. Find a friend you can trust to be honest with you—someone who will understand that you need him to be completely candid and open with his evaluation of you. You must also prepare yourself. If you expect your friend to be honest, you must be completely open and accepting of what you hear. The truth can often be brutal. I would refer you back to my aunt in Chapter one, whom I secretly recorded. When she heard herself played back, she thought she sounded like an old biddy. It is just such information about yourself that will be the most productive. Having a good "director" is invaluable to any performer. A good friend can serve that purpose.

Do you have a big nose, big feet? Are you a little too aggressive? Too timid? Do you stutter? Are you awkward, or clumsy? These are things that even your best friends are reluctant to tell you, and you are least likely to accept. Yet, they are the mother lode of comedy. Some of the funniest comics in the world are those who went through a very painful childhood as ugly ducklings. Since everyone laughed at them, they found acceptance by accepting the fact that they were funny. As we said at the very beginning, the saddest person in the world is one who can find nothing about himself at which to laugh.

Once you find those things about yourself that are funny, use them. If need be, over-exaggerate them so that the audience will recognize it as a spoof.

If you find it is too painful to poke fun directly at your personal character, there is another way. It is less painful, and sometimes may even be funnier, because it builds in comic contradictions. It involves poking fun at the person you would like to be.

If you are timid, try building a character that is aggressive or assertive. Try something like the Bob Hope braggart. Chances are your timidity will show through just enough to make a comic contradiction.

Certainly, this is the pattern around which the Minnie Pearl character of *Grand ole Opry* fame, is structured. In real life, She was a college graduate. Her real-life character had worked hard to transcend her country background, yet that background would have clung to her through the regional dialect of her early years. Her stage character used this contradiction well, striving to appear smart, clever and dressed up, but not quite being able to pull it off. The Tennessee dialect would cause the country ways to show through. Accenting this comedy contradiction, her trademark was a fancy hat with the price tag still dangling from it, like it was part of the decoration.

My own comic character was built in a similar pattern. Because of my low vision, my two juvenile offspring's claimed I was a walking disaster area. Not seeing well, I would accidentally knock things from the table, and crunch their prized-possessions under foot. It was almost certain that the same would happen on stage. Yet, I had always wanted to be a master magician, so the character began to develop. Affecting the style of the grand old masters, I used broad, theatrical gestures, and developed a melodramatic, commanding stage voice. At the same time, I allowed—even encouraged—my clumsiness to show through. Claiming that I would produce a rabbit from a hat, a cane would appear. Near-sightedly scrutinizing it in horror, I would make excuses for it. I grandly proclaimed that my white rabbit was wearing his black tuxedo. I proudly announced that, though he was a little skinny for a rabbit, it was because he was quite active in Weight Watchers.

Start with a few basic traits like this, and allow the character to grow. Gradually add more ideas until you find just the right combination of character qualities. Keep tabs on how exaggerated your character is becoming, and then match your material and timing to it.

PRESS SHIFT F5 FOR CHARACTER ALIGNMENT

Make it painless. If your character traits are those that can be especially distasteful to an audience, do something to sweeten it. Personally, I never cared much for Minnie Pearl. That is because I only heard her on the airwaves, and she did nothing audibly to convey the contradiction. I viewed her simply as a stupid country bumpkin, who was put on the air because she had a friend in the business. Had I been aware of the price tag dangling from the hat, I would have recognized it, at once, as a spoof. On the radio, she needed to include some obvious verbal cues like the dangling price tag. It needed more verbal exaggeration for me to get the point. It would have helped greatly if she would have used some specific audible comic devices like the malaprops and word distortions explained in Chapter Three.

As a performer, you must also believe completely in the character you are creating. If you believe he is real, so will your audience. From the inside of you, be serious about his reality. At the same time, you need to step outside of him and enjoy laughing at how delightfully funny he is. If you can silently chuckle at his silly foibles, your audience will see it, and laugh too. Billy Crystal, the comedian who creates so many comic characters—both imagined, and satires from real-life—says he considers them all to be close, personal friends of his.

Don't expect things to fall into place the first time. Test a few ideas on a trial audience. Present your character with firm, positive conviction. Suppose, for example, you are playing a timid character. Such a character would normally not be seen in front of an audience in the first place. If he were actually to do so, he would be too timid to speak up. Yet the audience must hear him. You must choose other traits to convey the timid ness. A stuttering, overly high-pitched, trembling voice might be selected, but played with plenty of volume and gusto.

In summary, to come off as natural and still be funny, you must have at least two reasons for everything you do. We have tried to emphasize that throughout. An actor does it when he walks over to stand on a trap door. His reason is to be there at a particular time. The audience believes he is only hanging up his coat. The magician does it

48   GET MORE LAUGHS FROM YOUR LAUGHS

when he reaches into his top hat. The audience believes he is reaching for his wand, and not actually ditching some telltale paper pellets. He must be only vaguely aware that the move hides his real reason.

The comic does it in a variety of different ways, pausing in obviously awkward places, moving in strange, unnatural ways, outrageously exaggerating all to get a laugh, but doing it under the umbrella of characterization. In that way, the audience will believe the unbelievable. They will believe that is the way he really is.

Each technique must be understood and mastered on its own, but cannot stand on its own. That is why comedy is so hard to do, and why it is so rewarding to the performer when he does it well.

For the seasoned performer, it can become as simple as working a computer keyboard. Just press the F key for character alignment.

EXERCISES:

1. Try on different characters for size. An easy way to do this is to find a joke book with stories in it that involve direct quotes: an old man, a man from Mars, an Indian, an Irishman, a little kid, etc. Practice telling the story by changing your manner of speech, and even your mannerisms, to convey the character as you quote him. Each time you tell the story, carry the character exaggeration a little farther. See how comfortable you can get, and how much the audience will accept, in the way of exaggeration.

2. Select one of the comic devices, such as *Slow Thinker,* as listed in Chapter Three. Write a short comic scenario, using this individual as the central character. Perhaps he is a professor in a college, or a deliveryman, looking for a particular address. To enhance his slow-thinking qualities, work in some of the other comic devices, such as the malaprop, word-distortion, non sequitur, twisted logic, or the literal meaning device. Be careful not to make it appear that he is simply stupid. This will cause an audience to resent the ridicule of someone who is

intellectually challenged. It will help with this problem, if you can build in a contradiction. As in the case of the professor, for example, make him so brilliant that he simply does not have time, or concern for the trivial. As in the case of the deliveryman, he can be simply trying very faithfully to follow the orders of a boss who has been careless about making his orders completely clear.

IN CONCLUSION

"Like a welcome summer rain, humor may suddenly cleanse and cool the earth, the air and you." Langston Hughes

"A sense of humor is part of the art of leadership, of getting along with people, of getting things done." Former president, Dwight D. Eisenhower.

Humor heals the spirit, lowers the blood pressure, makes friends of enemies, washes away long-standing animosities and clears out the cobwebs that clutter our lives. Use this wonderful treasure with wisdom and kindness. Whether you become a comic star or not, your life will be the richer for the effort.

APPENDIX

The Two Sides of Victor Borge video
   Distributed by Gurtman & Murtha Associates
   450 Seventh Avenue, Suite 2207 New York, NY 10123

Bruce "Charlie" Johnson
POB 82165, Kenmore WA 98028-0165
www.CharlieTheJugglingClown.com.

Old radio shows download
radiolovers.com/allshows

laughs.com

MARK TWAIN TONIGHT, a Hal Holbrook recording, outstanding source for study of the pause and timing

Andy Borowitz The Book of Shockers—Humorous New Year's Predictions

Klamm Magic LLC
1412 South Appleton Avenue
Independence MO 64052-3747
www.klamm-magic.com
klamm@klamm-magic.com

ABOUT THE AUTHOR

It is a truism that there are none so sad as those who cannot laugh at themselves. Bob Klamm has been laughing at himself for the last 75 years.

No one knew he was nearly blind—not even himself—until he was eight years old. He just kept on making jokes about his bumbling ways. He tells the whole story in his humorous and inspirational memoir, *Fly Like a Bumblebee*. He has recently written a stage play version of this prize-winning memoir.

R. W. (Bob) Klamm grew up in Kansas City, Kansas, where he was born nearly blind. In second grade, they gave him eyeglasses thick as Coke bottle bottoms—so heavy that Bob quips, "It was like the bottles were still attached."

In junior high school, he did his first big magic show for a student body of 500. At last! He was no longer an outcast. He was hooked on magic, and has been performing ever since.

The State Services for the Blind sent him to Northwestern University, where he graduated with honors, and a Bachelor's degree in drama, radio and TV.

At the age of 22 he returned to Kansas City, where he had the good fortune to stumble into what was probably the most creative advertising agency in the nation.

There, he pioneered the comedy radio commercial. It was in the early 50's, years before Garrison Keeler and the Smothers Brothers latched onto the idea. Some of Bob's original comedy radio writings are still available, now digitally enhanced and preserved on CD. The CD and his books are available on his web site.

Wanting to do more than just sell product, Bob went back to school for a Master's degree in Education, so that he could teach speech and drama in secondary schools. After earning his degree, he settled in for a twenty-year off-off-Broadway run of producing the best of professionally written Broadway comedies and dramas, as well as Shakespeare. It was at Van Horn High School, part of the Kansas City Missouri school system, located in Independence, Missouri. During this time he developed the techniques found in *Get More Laughs from Your Laughs.*

Bob is a master teacher, having shepherded numerous college students through their practice teaching. He teaches a comedy class for the University of Missouri at Kansas City in their Continuing Education division.

Operating Kansas City's oldest magic shop, Bob Klamm also sells his own magical inventions and other magic props to professional magicians and hobbyists, worldwide, on his web site at www.klamm-magic.com. Bob started a Kansas City assembly of the national Society of Young Magicians, and produced their annual magic show for 17 years. The Greater Kansas City Assembly #38 of the International Society of American Magicians bears his name.

Currently he is working on a book called *How To Out-Fox The Kids.* These are little "Pearls from the Klamm," sparkling little stories, fables, fractured fairy tales and sometimes humorous parables—little gems of wisdom designed to help your little gems of joy.

Bob and his wife, Berniece, live in Independence, Missouri, with a magic shop in the basement. They have two grown sons and four grand-daughters. There eldest, Dale, is Head Carpenter at Kansas City's Starlight Theater, a giant outdoor theater complex, where he is in charge of all that goes on back stage. Scott is a Chemical engineer, and does classified environmental studies for Midwest Research Institute. He plays a wide variety of musical instruments; and a major love of his is presenting folk music programs for local schools.

978-0-595-37373-4
0-595-37373-9

Lightning Source UK Ltd.
Milton Keynes UK
22 December 2009

147807UK00002B/342/A